GrowthSpurt

Also by Jerry Scott and Jim Borgman

Zits: Sketchbook 1

GrowthSpurt

Sketchbook 2

by JERRY SCOTT and JIM BORGMAN

**Andrews McMeel
Publishing**

Kansas City

To Kim and Lynn

Zits
by Jerry Scott and Jim Borgman

CHECK IT OUT!

HI JEREMY. HI HECTOR.

SARA??

YEAH, I KNOW, "COKE BOTTLES."

MY CONTACTS HAVE BEEN IRRITATING MY EYES, SO I HAVE TO WEAR MY GLASSES FOR A FEW DAYS.

IT'S A PAIN, BUT I HAVE NO CHOICE... SEE YOU LATER.

SEE YA.

BYE.

WHOA!

YEAH!

JUST WHEN I THOUGHT SHE COULDN'T GET ANY SEXIER...!

Zits
by JERRY SCOTT and JIM BORGMAN

DAD! ARE MY BLACK JEANS CLEAN?

HOW SHOULD I KNOW?

WELL, YOU'RE IN CHARGE OF THE LAUNDRY, AREN'T YOU?

JEREMY.... SON.... I WASH, DRY AND FOLD THE LAUNDRY.

I DO NOT TRACK IT BY TAGGING IT WITH ELECTRONIC BRACELETS AND MAP ITS MIGRATION PATTERNS.

JERRY SCOTT and JIM BORGMAN

NOR DO I FORM SEARCH-AND-RESCUE EFFORTS TO FIND IT WHEN IT IS LOST DEEP IN THE BRACKEN OF DUST BUNNIES, STALE DONUTS AND SNICKERS WRAPPERS UNDER YOUR DRESSER.

OR HIRE FIELD AGENTS TO KEEP IT UNDER 24-HOUR SURVEILLANCE SO THAT...

OK! OK! SHEESH! I'M SORRY I ASKED!

THAT WAS LAYING IT ON A LITTLE THICK, DON'T YOU THINK?

ACTUALLY, I MAY TRY THAT TAGGING IDEA...

SO, I HEAR THERE'S A FRESHMAN CLASS PARTY AT ASHLEY'S NEXT WEEKEND.

ARE YOU PLANNING ON ASKING ANYONE SPECIAL?

I'M NOT AT LIBERTY TO SAY.

OH WELL, NICE TRY.

THAT WAS A 'YES', DEAR.

JERRY SCOTT & JIM BORGMAN

MMP!

HANG ON...

UM.

TUH!

I DON'T APPRECIATE YOU EAVESDROPPING ON MY CONVERSATIONS, MOM!

DON'T WORRY, MY LIPS ARE SEALED.

I'M REALLY GETTING PSYCHED ABOUT DVD TECHNOLOGY!

WHAT ABOUT YOU, DAD?

UMM...

JERRY SCOTT and JIM BORGMAN

YOU DO KNOW ABOUT DVD...? PLEASE TELL ME THAT YOU KNOW ABOUT DVD!

EVERYBODY KNOWS ABOUT DVD!

OF COURSE I KNOW ABOUT DVD! SHEESH! GIVE YOUR OLD MAN A LITTLE CREDIT!

WHEW!

DONUT VALUE DEAL... RIGHT?

YOU MARCH RIGHT BACK IN THERE AND FESS UP.

JEREMY! YOU'RE WEARING A PONYTAIL! HOW CUTE!

JERRY SCOTT and JIM BORGMAN

WHAT THE HECK ARE YOU SUPPOSED TO BE??

MUCH BETTER...

YAWN!

'MORNING, JEREMY

I THINK I LEFT MY ROBE IN THE DRYER.

JERRY SCOTT and JIM BORGMAN

WHAT'S WITH HIM?

I DON'T KNOW... SOMETHING ABOUT A GENE POOL.

BIG DAWG

JEREMY, I FOUND THE ELECTRICAL TAPE IN MY TOOLBOX, LIKE YOU SAID.

I'M SORRY I ACCUSED YOU OF NOT RETURNING IT... YOU WERE ACTUALLY RIGHT AND I WAS WRONG.

"ACTUALLY"??

JERRY SCOTT and JIM BORGMAN

PRITHEE, SON...

...IF 'TIS FORTHRIGHT DELIVERY OF THINE SOUL INTO THE HANDS OF BEELZEBUB THOU SEEKETH, METHINKS THOU HAST DIVINED A METHOD OF UNFAILING CERTAINTY.

JERRY SCOTT and JIM BORGMAN

FOR PETE'S SAKE, MOM, DON'T BE SUCH A PRUDE. IT'S JUST 'SOUTH PARK'!

HEY, JEREMY! SAVE SOME HOT WATER FOR THE REST OF US!

LET'S GO!

HURRY IT UP!

THAT SHOWER HAS BEEN RUNNING FOR TWENTY MINUTES

KNOCK! KNOCK! KNOCK!

OH, THAT'S RIGHT! I FORGOT!

'SCUSE ME, DAD.

HONEY, DO YOU HEAR A BANGING SOUND?

BANG BANG BANG BANG BANG

JERRY SCOTT & JIM BORGMAN

I CAN'T BELIEVE HOW MUCH TIME YOU WASTE JUST LYING AROUND, JEREMY!

JERRY SCOTT and JIM BORGMAN

WHEN I WAS YOUR AGE, I WAS OUT PLAYING BALL OR FORMING STUDY GROUPS OR TALKING WITH MY FRIENDS...

YEAH. AND LOOK AT YOU NOW.

GROUNDED?? FOR WHAT?

I'M NOT SURE... IT ALL HAPPENED PRETTY FAST.

I THOUGHT THE BAND WAS GOING TO PRACTICE TONIGHT

TIM CANCELED... HE HAS HOMEWORK.

WE'RE THINKING ABOUT KICKING HIM OUT OF THE BAND.

THAT'S KIND OF HARSH, ISN'T IT?

SHOW A LITTLE COMPASSION! TIM IS AN IMPORTANT PART OF THE GROUP, ISN'T HE?

YEAH, I GUESS SO.

...PLUS HE OWNS THE AMPLIFIER.

ON THE OTHER HAND, IF HE ISN'T RELIABLE...

JERRY SCOTT and JIM BORGMAN

UM....

SHHH! I'M TELEPATHICALLY COMMUNICATING WITH THIS FLY!

I'M TELLING IT TO LEAVE THIS BOWL OF FRUIT ALONE AND GO SOMEWHERE ELSE.

JERRY SCOTT and JIM BORGMAN

PIFF!

UH-OH... NOTHING BUT STATIC.

OH MAN, I'M WIPED! I'M HEADING FOR BED.

I'VE BEEN RUNNING ON FUMES ALL EVENING.

JERRY SCOTT and JIM BORGMAN

....WHICH, IN HIS CASE, CAN BE SUBSTANTIAL!

I'M GOING TO PRETEND I DIDN'T HEAR THAT.

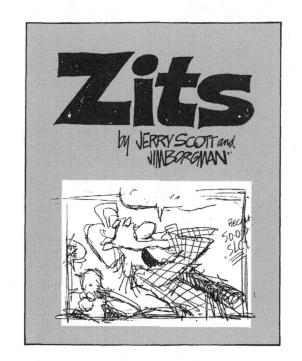

I'LL NEVER LET GO, JACK! (SOB!) I'LL NEVER LET GO!

ON THE OTHER HAND, THAT GUY CLINGING TO THE WOODEN BARREL OVER THERE IS KINDA CUTE....

JERRY SCOTT and JIM BORGMAN

SO SARA DOESN'T EVEN TAKE YOU SERIOUSLY IN YOUR DREAMS??

I EITHER NEED A NEW GIRLFRIEND OR SOME NEW FANTASIES.

WHAT'S WRONG, JEREMY? YOU LOOK LIKE YOU'VE BEEN HIT BY A TRUCK!

WORSE!

JERRY SCOTT and JIM BORGMAN

MOM REFUSED TO GIVE ME A NOTE SO I COULD SKIP THE HEALTH FAIR, SO I MISSED MY RIDE WITH TIM and HAD TO WALK HOME IN THE STUPID RAIN BECAUSE SHE WAS TOO "BUSY" TO PICK ME UP!

THAT'S ALMOST AN **HOUR** OF MY TIME **WASTED** ON UNNECESSARY PHYSICAL ACTIVITY!

I'LL GO HAVE A FEW WORDS WITH HER.

WAY TO GO!

JEREMY, I THOUGHT WE HAD A POLICY AGAINST WATCHING TV BEFORE YOUR HOMEWORK IS FINISHED.

OH.

WELL, I'M PROPOSING AN AMENDMENT TO THE POLICY...

...I THINK THERE SHOULD BE EXCEPTIONS ALLOWED, SUCH AS WHEN A NEW X-FILES EPISODE IS ON.

JERRY SCOTT JIM BORGMAN

AH! SO, IN OTHER WORDS, THE POLICY SHOULD STAND EXCEPT WHEN YOU FIND IT INCONVENIENT!

BRILLIANT!

THANKS, MOM... I KNEW YOU WOULD UNDERSTAND.

THAT WAS SARCASM!

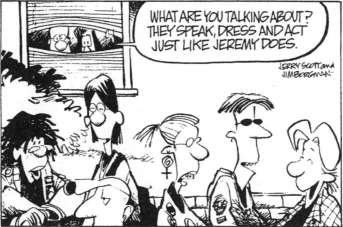

28

HEY, MOM, HECTOR AND I ARE THINKING ABOUT GETTING SUMMER JOBS AS LIFEGUARDS.

GUYS! THAT'S A SUPER IDEA!

YOU'RE BOTH GREAT SWIMMERS AND YOU'LL GET TO LEARN CPR!

I'M PROUD OF YOU BOTH FOR TAKING ON RESPONSIBILITY AND GIVING BACK TO YOUR COMMUNITY.

JERRY SCOTT and JIM BORGMAN

WOW. YOUR MOM CAN EVEN MAKE GETTING PAID FOR WATCHING GIRLS SOUND LIKE WORK!

IT'S HER GIFT

JERRY SCOTT and JIM BORGMAN

BIP! BEEP! BOOP!

I TOLD YOU BEFORE, JEREMY... THEY DON'T LOOK AT THE SECURITY TAPES UNLESS THERE'S A PROBLEM.

THEIR LOSS.

IT'S KIND OF QUIET UP THERE... WHY DON'T YOU GO SEE WHAT JEREMY IS DOING.

OKAY.

WHAT ARE YOU DOING?

ADDING A COUPLE OF HOT LINKS AND JAVASCRIPTING MY HOME PAGE.

JERRY SCOTT and JIM BORGMAN

WELL?

SOMETHING ABOUT SAUSAGE AND COFFEE.

31

ARE YOU REALLY GOING TO BUY DAD A NOSE HAIR TRIMMER FOR FATHER'S DAY?

IT'S WHAT HE WANTS.

I KNOW, BUT IS THAT A REASON?

MAYBE WE'RE NOT THINKING OUTSIDE THE BOX HERE.

A FATHER'S DAY GIFT SHOULD BE SOMETHING UNEXPECTED! SOMETHING REMARKABLE!

SOMETHING THAT TRANSCENDS TRADITION AND VENTURES INTO THE REALM OF AWESOME-NESS!

IN OTHER WORDS, SOMETHING THAT YOU WANT TO BORROW.

I'VE TAKEN THE LIBERTY OF PREPARING THIS LIST OF ALTERNATIVES.

WE MADE IT TO SUMMER, MAN! WHAT'S OUR PLAN?

WELL...

...I WAS THINKING HAVE LUNCH, WATCH A VIDEO, HANG OUT.

NO. I'M TALKING ABOUT THE WHOLE SUMMER.

SO AM I.

WALT! CHAD FOUND A SUMMER JOB NEAR HOME!

AND THEY'RE GOING TO GIVE HIM A COMPANY CAR!

AND HIS OWN OFFICE!

AND A PARKING SPACE!

AND THEY'RE GOING TO PAY HIM MORE THAN YOU MAKE.

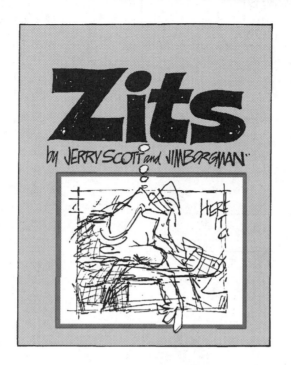

Zits

by JERRY SCOTT and JIM BORGMAN

HI, JEREMY! IS THIS YOUR MOM?

HI. UH.... YEAH.

HI.... I'M SYLVIA CATLEY, JEREMY'S MATH TEACHER.

OH! HI!

HE'S FUNNY.... HE'S POLITE.... HE'S TALKATIVE....

I WISH I HAD A WHOLE ROOMFUL OF JEREMYS!

I JUST WANTED TO TELL YOU WHAT AN ABSOLUTE **JOY** IT IS TO HAVE JEREMY IN MY CLASS.

REALLY? MY JEREMY?

JUST THOUGHT YOU'D LIKE TO KNOW...

YES! GOSH! THANKS!

HERE IT COMES....

OKAY... WHO ARE YOU, AND WHAT HAVE YOU DONE WITH MY SON??

JERRY SCOTT and JIM BORGMAN

JEREMY, THIS IS HOW I WANT TO GET MY HAIR CUT.

SEE, THE CURL WOULD HELP SOFTEN MY FEATURES, AND THE WEDGE MIGHT MAKE MY NECK LOOK LONGER AND MORE GRACEFUL. WHAT DO YOU THINK?

JERRY SCOTT and JIMBORGMAN

WHAT DO I THINK ABOUT **WHAT**?

@!#☆○✕ "Y" CHROMOSOME!

ARE YOU SERIOUS ABOUT GETTING A NEW HAIRSTYLE, MOM?

I THINK IT'S ABOUT TIME, DON'T YOU?

PSST! PSST! PSST!

JERRY SCOTT and JIMBORGMAN

IT'S HARD TO IMAGINE THAT YOU COULD LOOK ANY BETTER THAN YOU ALREADY DO, BUT IF IT MAKES YOU HAPPY, GO FOR IT!

WHAT A SWEET THING TO SAY, JEREMY!

MASTER!

YOU LEARNED WELL, GRASSHOPPER!

JERRY SCOTT and JIMBORGMAN

LOVE YOUR NEW HAIRSTYLE.

REALLY? YOU'RE NOT JUST SAYING THAT?

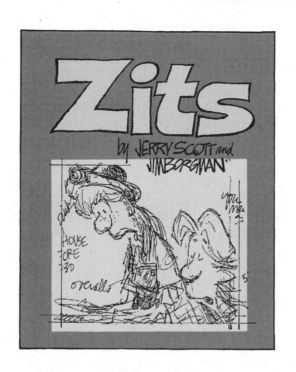

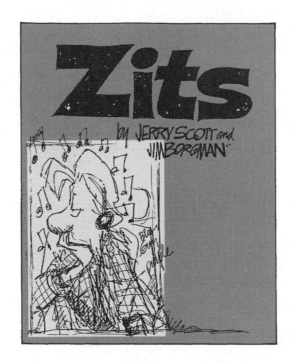

Zits
by Jerry Scott and Jim Borgman

So, how's everything going at school, son?

I hear that Martians landed in New Jersey this morning.

Oh, hey! Your mom and I are thinking about upgrading your computer with more of those gigathingies... interested?

You know, if you want me to, I'll hire a lawn service to cut the grass so you don't have to waste your valuable youth on such menial labor.

By the way... the next time the band practices at our house, do me a favor and turn the amps up all the way, OK?

Absolutely, definitely and you got it.

...but the Martian thing sounds kind of unlikely.

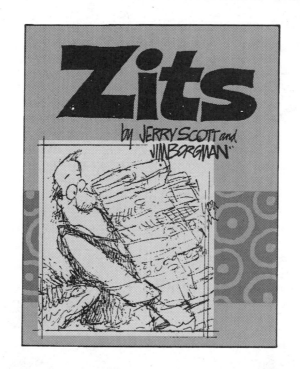

Coping Effectively with your Teen

by Connie Duncan, Ph.D.

WATCH IT!

TAP TAP TAPPA-TAP TAPPA TAP

GIVE IT BACK, JERKFACE!

YOU HAD THE REMOTE LAST NIGHT!

YOU SET IT DOWN!

BUT YOU KNEW I WAS COMING RIGHT BACK!

OOOH... TOUGH GUY!

THAT DOES IT!

KNOCK IT OFF!

Chapter One: Communication

TAPPA TAP-A-TAP TAPPA-TAP-A TAP

THIS IS THE COOLEST SONG.

I CAN TOTALLY RELATE TO IT.

UH, JEREMY... THIS TUNE IS ABOUT A GUY WHO GETS SO BUMMED OUT AFTER TAKING A WAD OF DRUGS THAT HE GOUGES HIS EYES OUT WITH A GARDEN RAKE!

HOW CAN YOU POSSIBLY RELATE TO THAT??

HEY! I HAVE PROBLEMS, TOO!

SPEAKING OF GARDEN RAKES... REMEMBER, THE LAWN NEEDS MOWING.

THIS WEEK TOTALLY BIT!

"BIT"?

OKAY, THIS WEEK BITED!

THAT CAN'T BE RIGHT, EITHER.

THIS WEEK HAS TOTALLY BITTEN?

ALMOST... BUT NOT QUITE.

BACK ON MONDAY, I DIDN'T KNOW THIS WEEK WAS GOING TO BITE SO BAD!

I HATE CONJUGATING IRREGULAR VULGARITIES.

51

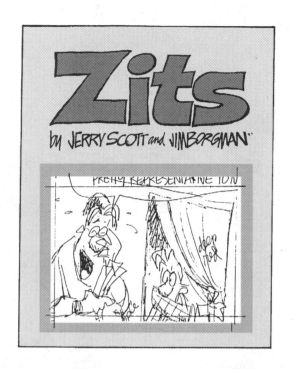

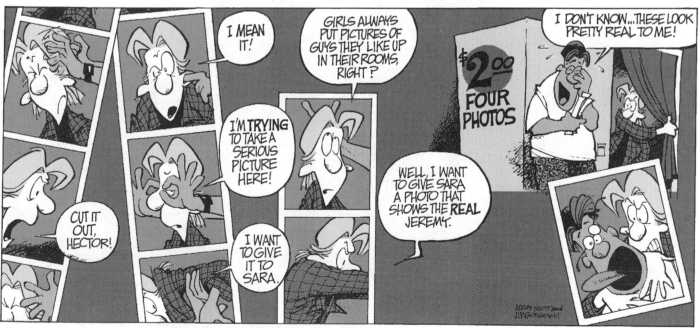

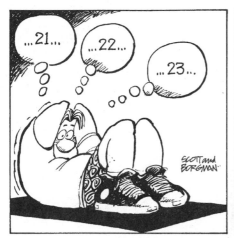

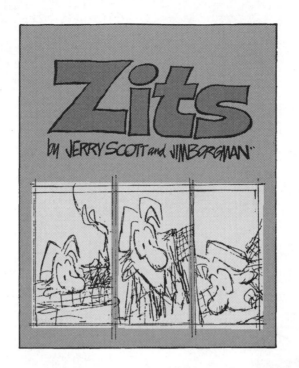

60

61

HECTOR! WE DID IT, MAN! WE GOT AWAY WITH IT!

WHAT WAS THAT NOISE?

WE ACTUALLY STOLE A STREET SIGN! YESSS!

QUIET! I THINK I HEAR VOICES!

THIS IS SO COOL!

SHHH! WAS THAT A SIREN?

"I ADMIT THE DEED! TEAR UP THE PLANKS! HERE! HERE! IT IS THE BEATING OF HIS HIDEOUS HEART!"
The Telltale Heart - Edgar Allen Poe

SOMETIMES I DON'T UNDERSTAND A WORD YOU SAY.

JEREMY ST.

SCOTT and BORGMAN

SO WHAT DO YOU INTEND TO DO WITH THE STREET SIGN THAT YOU STOLE?

WE STOLE.

I THOUGHT IT WOULD LOOK GOOD HERE IN THE VAN.

OF COURSE, WE'LL HAVE TO MAKE SURE OUR PARENTS NEVER SEE IT...

AND IF SARA FINDS OUT, SHE'LL FREAK...

AND WE'LL HAVE TO HIDE IT WHEN WE TAKE THE VAN TO BE SERVICED.

SCOTT and BORGMAN

JEREMY ST.

HOW CAN SOMETHING SO COOL MAKE YOU FEEL SO GUILTY?

YOU TURNED THE STOLEN STREET SIGN INTO THE POLICE?? WHO-O-OA!

I HAD TO! IT WAS DRIVING ME CRAZY WITH GUILT!

BUT I PROMISE YOU, HECTOR, THAT WAS THE LAST DISHONEST ACT OF MY LIFE!

SCOTT and BORGMAN

WAIT. TURNING A PIECE OF STOLEN PROPERTY IN TO THE POLICE ISN'T A DISHONEST ACT.

NO, BUT USING YOUR NAME WAS.

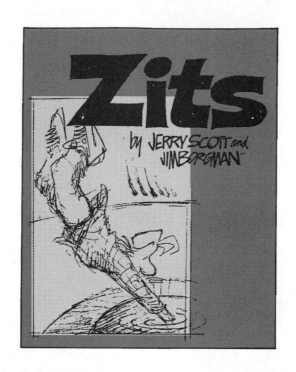

So, there we were... finally on stage.

Everything seemed like it was happening in SLOW MOTION and FAST MOTION at the same time.

And when it was over, I looked at Hector, and we both knew something very big had happened....

We didn't TANK!

When we finished the song, everybody was cheering and I heard Sara call my name.

YEAH! CLAP! CLAP!

JEREMY?

WOOO!

It was then that I received the SECOND-BEST COMPLIMENT OF MY LIFE...

YOU GUYS WEREN'T THAT BAD!

...FOLLOWED BY the FIRST-BEST.

THIS IS INCREDIBLE!

I'M ACTUALLY KISSING SARA...

...AND IT WAS HER IDEA.

WELL, HEY, I GOTTA GO.

'K

YESS! IT FINALLY HAPPENED!

HECTOR IS NOT GOING TO BELIEVE IT WHEN I TELL HIM ABOUT...

...THIS.

When I saw Hector in a lip clench with that girl, I couldn't believe my eyes!

OH, UH... MINDY, THIS IS JEREMY. JEREMY, THIS IS MINDY.

MANDY.

SORRY. MANDY.

EASY TO MEET YOU.

Then I couldn't believe my mouth.

I MEAN, NICE TO MEET YOU.

SO, DO YOU LIVE AROUND HERE, MANDY?

WHERE DO YOU GO TO SCHOOL?

ARE YOU A FRESHMAN?

WAIT! SORRY.... I DIDN'T MEAN TO GRILL YOU LIKE THAT.

HECTOR CAN TELL ME ALL ABOUT YOU LATER.

YEAH...

SCOTT and BORGMAN

...THAT IS, IF I TELL HIM...

HUUUUUUUHH...

SIGH-H-H-H-H

SCOTT and BORGMAN

I HAVE THE FEELING THAT "SUMMER BOREDOM" MAY HAVE FINALLY SET IN.

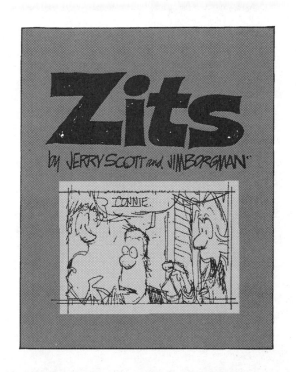

JEREMY ST
DON'T EVEN BREATHE...
IF WE DON DIE, REMIN ME TO KILL YO
YOU GUYS WEREN'T THAT BAD!
SHOULD THEY SAY SOMETHING?
MISS YOU.
4 EVER
OH, UH... MINDY, THIS IS JEREMY. JEREMY, THIS IS MINDY.
MANDY.
SORRY, MANDY.
MISS YOU.
BE STRONG
203
204
BUT... BUT... BUT...

OKAY, LET'S GO IN AND SEE HOW THESE FIT.

DRESSING ROOMS

SCOTT and BORGMAN

I MEAN, **YOU** GO IN AND SEE HOW THESE FIT.

THAT'S MORE LIKE IT.

HEY, MR. BLACKWELL, WHERE'D YOU PICK UP THE DWEEBWEAR?

MY AUNT PATTY SENT IT AND MY MOM'S MAKING ME WEAR IT!

SCOTT and BORGMAN

SHE KNOWS PERFECTLY WELL I'M UNCOMFORTABLE WEARING STUFF LIKE THIS!

WHAT, POLYESTER?

NO. CO-ORDINATED!

YOU KNOW **MY** MOTTO: IF IT GOES, IT BLOWS!

HELLOO?

IS JEREMY THERE?

NO, BUT HE SHOULD BE BACK IN ABOUT AN HOUR....

CAN I TAKE A MESSAGE?

NO

OKAY

SCOTT and BORGMAN

...I'LL HOLD.

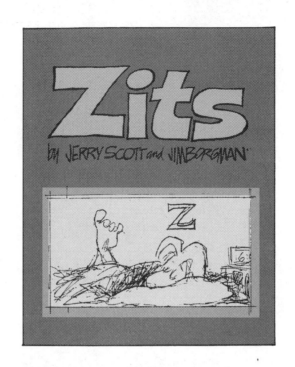

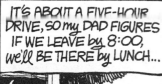

WE'RE SUPPOSED TO LEAVE in the MORNING to TAKE my BROTHER CHAD BACK to NOTRE DAME.

IT'S ABOUT A FIVE-HOUR DRIVE, SO my DAD FIGURES IF WE LEAVE by 8:00, WE'LL BE THERE by LUNCH...

...BARRING ANY UNFORESEEN DELAYS.

READY?

HONK! HONK!

Z

SCOTT and BORGMAN

TURN IT DOWN, JERKWAD!

I'M USING HEADPHONES, DIPSTICK!

DEAL WITH IT, BUTTMUNCH!

I CAN STILL HEAR IT, YOU SKANK!

SCOTT and BORGMAN

SOME THINGS NEVER CHANGE, DO THEY?

I USED TO PULL OVER AND YELL AT THEM, BUT NOW I'M AFRAID THEY'D JUST DRIVE OFF WITHOUT US.

MORON!

BONE-HEAD!

THIS IS AWESOME!

I LOVE COLLEGE CAMPUSES! LET'S WALK AROUND AND BLEND IN WITH THE STUDENTS.

LOOK OLDER... LOOK OLDER

LOOK YOUNGER... LOOK YOUNGER...

SCOTT and BORGMAN

75

FLY TRUE, MY ORANGE PEBBLED ORB, FOR VICTORY IS WITHIN OUR GRASP.

SEEK THY TARGET AND LET THE WORLD RESOUND WITH THE ZING OF COTTON STRING!

THIS IS WHY OUR GAMES OF H·O·R·S·E LAST LONGER THAN MOST CHESS TOURNAMENTS

SHH! YOU'RE BREAKING MY CONCENTRATION!

COME ON, JEREMY! THAT SHOT IS IMPOSSIBLE!

I CAN MAKE THIS! I'VE MADE IT BEFORE!

THE ONLY TIME YOU EVER MADE A BEHIND-THE-BACK, LEFT-HANDED, HALF-COURT SHOT WE WERE IN SEVENTH GRADE!

IT WAS DURING RECESS ON A WINDY DAY, AND THE ONLY REASON IT WENT IN THE HOOP IS BECAUSE IT BOUNCED OFF SOMEBODY ELSE'S BALL IN MIDAIR!

SO, YOU CONCEDE THAT IT'S POSSIBLE.

I CONCEDE THAT YOU'RE AN IDIOT.

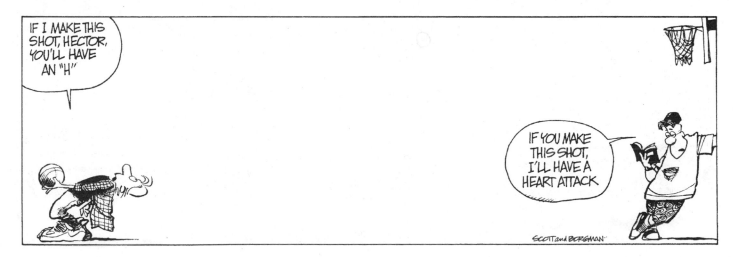

IF I MAKE THIS SHOT, HECTOR, YOU'LL HAVE AN "H"

IF YOU MAKE THIS SHOT, I'LL HAVE A HEART ATTACK

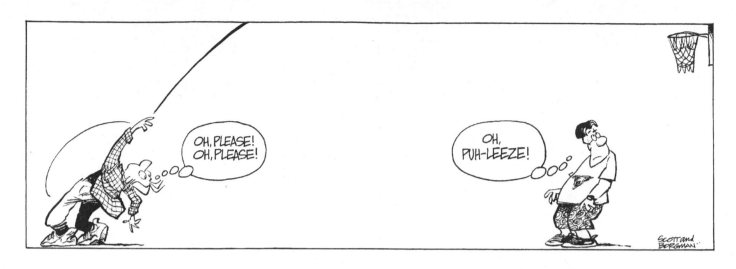

Zits
by JERRY SCOTT and JIM BORGMAN

JEREMY, HAVE YOU SEEN MY CAR KEYS?

I THOUGHT I LEFT THEM ON MY DRESSER, BUT NOW I WONDER IF YOUR DAD PICKED THEM UP BY MISTAKE. WAIT— I BET THEY'RE IN MY COAT POCKET.

BUT I DROPPED THAT OFF AT THE CLEANERS, SO HOW COULD I HAVE DRIVEN HOME? THAT DOESN'T MAKE ANY SENSE...OH, SHOOT! I FORGOT TO BRING THEM MY YELLOW DRESS AND YOUR DAD'S SPORTCOAT.

NOW I'LL HAVE TO SWING BY THERE ON MY WAY TO THE POST OFFICE AND, OH, HERE ARE MY KEYS RIGHT IN MY HAND! NEVER MIND.

BYE!

HOW DID THESE PEOPLE EVER SURVIVE IN HIGH SCHOOL?

AHHH! AFTER A LONG, HARD DAY, IT'S GOOD TO STRETCH OUT IN MY LIVING ROOM ON MY FURNITURE AND WATCH MY TELEVISION FOR WHICH I HAVE WORKED SO HARD TO PROVIDE FOR MY FAMILY!

SCOTT and BORGMAN

THE IRONY JUST ESCAPES YOU, DOESN'T IT?

SAY AGAIN?

HERE'S AN ARTICLE ABOUT A FAMILY IN ALASKA THAT WAS DRIVING ALONG WHEN THEY HIT A MOOSE!

SCOTT and BORGMAN

THE CAR MUST HAVE BEEN GOING PRETTY FAST BECAUSE MOOSE PARTS CAME CRASHING THROUGH THE WINDSHIELD and SPLATTERED ALL OVER THEM!

I WONDER IF IT TOTALED THE CAR?

HOW COULD THAT HAVE BEEN PREVENTED?

WHY DOESN'T ANYTHING COOL LIKE THAT EVER HAPPEN TO US?

I HATE IT WHEN THESE OLD FOGIES WRITE ADVICE BOOKS FOR TEENAGERS.

"TEEN TALK"... SPARE ME!

LOOK AT THIS GUY'S PICTURE! HE MUST BE AT LEAST THIRTY!

"CHAPTER 1. PARENTS ARE PEOPLE, TOO"

WHAT DOES HE HAVE TO SAY THAT COULD POSSIBLY INTEREST OUR GENERATION?

"CHAPTER 5. TEN THINGS THAT TURN GIRLS ON."

SCOTT & BORGMAN

UH, SARA? REMEMBER WHEN MY BAND FINISHED PLAYING AT the BATTLE OF THE GARAGE BANDS AND YOU CAME UP AND KISSED ME?

YEAH

WELL, I WAS JUST... YOU KNOW, THAT, UH... I MEAN...UM... WOW, YOU KNOW?

I SENSE A DEEP EMOTIONAL BOND.

IS ENGLISH REALLY YOUR PRIMARY LANGUAGE?

JEREMY, FOR THE NINETEENTH TIME, WOULD YOU--

OKAY, MOM! OKAY! I GOT IT!

YOU DON'T HAVE TO KEEP TELLING ME OVER AND OVER, ALL RIGHT? IT'S ANNOYING, DEMEANING AND TOTALLY UNNECESSARY.

FINE! THEN JUST DO IT!

DO WHAT?

NOW I FORGET, TOO.

HEY, JEREMY.... HOW DO YOU THINK I'D LOOK WITH CONTACTS?

LIKE THE TOP OF A PEPPER SHAKER

THAT'S WHAT I WAS AFRAID OF.

SCOTT and BORGMAN

I CAN'T BELIEVE YOU'RE SAYING THAT WE SHOULD PAY FOR JEREMY'S INSURANCE, GAS **AND** CAR PAYMENTS WHEN HE GETS HIS LICENSE!

HE HAS US OVER A BARREL!

I'LL NEVER GET ANYWHERE ON MY BOOK IF I HAVE TO KEEP DRIVING HIM TO BAND PRACTICE, MALLS and VIDEO STORES!

UM-HMM.

...AND YOU'VE LOST DOZENS OF OFFICE HOURS TAKING HIM TO SUMMER JOBS, LIBRARIES and AFTER-SCHOOL EVENTS.

TRUE.

KENYON

IF YOU ASK ME, JEREMY'S DRIVER'S LICENSE IS GOING TO BENEFIT **US** MORE THAN HIM!

I WISH WE HAD BEEN **MY** PARENTS WHEN **I** WAS SIXTEEN!

YOU KNOW, YOU'RE RIGHT! WE PARENTS ARE THE ONES WHO **REALLY** BENEFIT WHEN OUR KIDS LEARN TO DRIVE...

...AND YET WE'VE MANAGED TO CONVINCE OUR TEENAGERS THAT WE **DREAD** THE DAY THEY LEARN!

SCOTT and BORGMAN

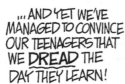

IT'S LIKE A VAST PARENTAL CONSPIRACY!

BUT IT ONLY WORKS AS LONG AS THE SECRET IS NEVER BETRAYED.

I'LL NEVER TELL.

MY LIPS ARE SEALED.

HELLO.

MOM, I REALLY, REALLY, REALLY WANT A PAGER.

WELL, I REALLY, REALLY, REALLY DON'T WANT TO GET YOU ONE.

BUT I REALLY, REALLY, REALLY NEED ONE!

THEN GO WORK REALLY, REALLY, REALLY HARD AND EARN THE MONEY TO BUY ONE.

SO, ARE YOU GETTING A PAGER?

REALLY, REALLY, REALLY DOUBTFUL

SCOTT and BORGMAN

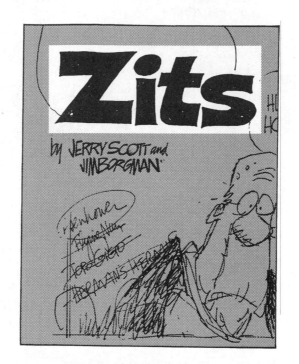

Zits

by JERRY SCOTT and JIM BORGMAN

JIMMY CARTER... DISCO... WATERGATE...

ELVIS... NEIL ARMSTRONG... THE BRADY BUNCH...

LEISURE SUITS... NEHRU JACKETS... BELL BOTTOMS...

ED SULLIVAN... DOBIE GILLIS...

JFK...

HULA HOOPS... EISENHOWER... BLACK AND WHITE TELEVISION...

...ALL THAT IN YOUR LO-O-ONG, FULL LIFETIME.

STEADY... HE'S JUST TRYING TO PSYCHE YOU OUT...

WHAT'S THE MATTER, DAD? DO I SENSE A LITTLE FATIGUE?

JEREMY, YOU CAN'T BE SERIOUS ABOUT THIS!

CAN'T I?

MY MOM IS A PSYCHOLOGIST WHO USED TO WORK WITH DISTURBED KIDS ALL THE TIME...

...ALL I HAVE TO DO IS ACT A LITTLE TWISTED AND SHE'LL DO ANYTHING IT TAKES TO BRING ME BACK TO NORMAL!

(GASP!) IF I BUY A MARILYN MANSON CD, THEY MIGHT SEND ME TO EUROPE!

IF YOU START WEARING THAT DOG COLLAR, I HOPE YOU **MOVE** TO EUROPE!

HI, MOM

JEREMY? IS THAT A DOG COLLAR YOU'RE WEARING?

YEAH.

I'VE BEEN THINKING ABOUT HANGING OUT WITH A BAD CROWD AND I THOUGHT THIS MIGHT HELP ME FIT IN.

MY COMPUTER IS ALMOST OBSOLETE, SO INSTEAD OF ASKING YOU TO BUY ME A NEW ONE, I'M EXPLORING DARKER, LESS WHOLESOME INTERESTS.

SEE YA

DO YOU THINK SHE GOT THE MESSAGE?

OH, NO. YOU WERE MUCH TOO SUBTLE.

...AND THEN JEREMY WALKS IN WEARING A **DOG COLLAR**!

A DOG COLLAR??

YES! YOU KNOW WHAT THAT MEANS, DON'T YOU?

WELL, OF COURSE! IT'S OBVIOUS!

HE'S FALLING IN WITH THE WRONG CROWD!

I WAS GOING TO GUESS THAT HE WANTS A PUPPY.

Zits

by Jerry Scott and Jim Borgman

CASH AGAIN?? HAVE THEY NO IMAGINATION?

HI, SWEETIE

HEY, MOM. WHAT'S UP?

NOT MUCH. I JUST FINISHED YOUR BIOLOGY HOMEWORK FOR YOU.

COOL. DON'T FORGET THAT ESSAY ON 'BEOWULF.' CHOP CHOP!

OH, ANOTHER RECORD COMPANY CALLED AND OFFERED YOUR BAND A RECORDING CONTRACT WITH A $2,000,000 BONUS.

CASH AGAIN?? HAVE THEY NO IMAGINATION?

THE STATE LEGISLATURE CHANGED THE DRIVING AGE TO FIFTEEN. HERE'S A SET OF CAR KEYS FOR YOU.

THE FERRARI? THANKS!

LET'S SEE...THE NEW BIG SCREEN TV YOUR DAD BOUGHT IS TOO BIG FOR THE DEN, SO WE'RE HAVING IT MOVED UP HERE TO YOUR ROOM.

STEADY

OH, AND YOU MIGHT HAVE TROUBLE GETTING INTO THE BATHROOM FOR THE NEXT FEW MONTHS BECAUSE THE SWEDISH WOMEN'S OLYMPIC GYMNASTICS TEAM IS MOVING INTO CHAD'S OLD BEDROOM.

I'LL MANAGE.

HI!

THERE HE GOES, GIGGLING IN HIS SLEEP AGAIN!

WHY DOES THAT ALWAYS MAKE ME UNEASY?

HEH HEH HEH

SCOTT AND BORGMAN

Zits
by Jerry Scott and Jim Borgman

DON'T MIND ME, KIDS... I'M JUST LOOKING FOR A SNACK.

ARE YOU SURE YOU TWO HAVE ENOUGH LIGHT IN HERE TO STUDY?

YES.

IT'S FINE, MOM.

PAPER CLIPS.... PAPER CLIPS...

AHH! GOOD OLD WATER!

SCOTT and BORGMAN

TSK! WHEN'S THE LAST TIME ANYBODY DUSTED THE TOP OF THIS REFRIGERATOR?

DO YOUR PARENTS ALWAYS SPEND THIS MUCH TIME WALKING IN AND OUT OF THE KITCHEN, JEREMY?

ONLY WHEN THEY WANT TO HUMILIATE ME.

SNI-I-I-I-I-I-FF!

SMACK! SMACK! YES, I THINK THIS BOTTLE WILL DO NICELY.

I GOTTA HAND IT TO YOU, HECTOR...

NOBODY KNOWS YOO-HOO LIKE YOU DO.

HOW TRUE.

SCOTT and BORGMAN

MAN, WHEN WE TURN SIXTEEN, IT'S "HELLO, DRIVER'S LICENSE!"

OH YEAH!

AND ONCE WE CAN DRIVE, IT'S "HELLO, INDEPENDENCE!"

AND ONCE WE'RE INDEPENDENT, IT'S "HELLO, WORLD!"

SCOTT and BORGMAN

SNIFF!

TUCKED INSIDE EVERY HELLO IS A LITTLE GOODBYE.

TALK ABOUT RUDE!

REALLY!

SCOTT and BORGMAN

THOSE PEOPLE RUINED THE MOVIE FOR ME.

ALL THEY DID WAS COMPLAIN! COMPLAIN! COMPLAIN!

THERE WERE SCENES WHERE I COULD BARELY HEAR MYSELF TALKING!

NEXT TIME I'LL COMPLAIN TO THE MANAGER.

HE'S IN MY ALGEBRA CLASS.

HEAVENS TO MURGATROYD!!

DAD! HOLD IT... DON'T MOVE!

OKAY... SAY THAT AGAIN. INTO THE MICROPHONE.

WHAT? "HEAVENS TO MURGATROYD"?

PERFECT. NOW SMILE.

THANK YOU.

FLASH!

HEY, MOM! I GOT MY REPORT ON DEAD LANGUAGES HALF-FINISHED!

NOW WAIT JUST A GOSH-DARN PEA-PICKIN' MINUTE!

LOOK, JEREMY! ISN'T THAT YOUR FRIEND SARA? I DIDN'T KNOW SHE HAD HER LEARNER'S PERMIT!

HI, SARA! I'M JUST TAKING JEREMY TO HIS BAND PRACTICE.

NO, HE STILL DOESN'T DRIVE!

HE WON'T BE 16 FOR A WHILE YET!

HEY! MAYBE YOU COULD GIVE HIM A DRIVING LESSON SOMEDAY!

BETTER YET... WHY DON'T I JUST LIE DOWN IN THE ROAD AND LET HER BACK THE CAR OVER ME REPEATEDLY.

RECENTLY, LIKE IN THE LAST TEN YEARS, I'VE NOTICED THAT MY HAIR HAS BEEN THINNING.

YEAH. TIME SURE FLIES.

RECENTLY, LIKE IN THE LAST TEN YEARS, I'VE NOTICED THAT TWO-THIRDS OF MY LIFE HAS PASSED BY.

SCOTT and BORGMAN

Zits by JERRY SCOTT and JIM BORGMAN™

LADIES AND GENTLEMEN, THE TRIUMPHANT RETURN OF THE HOT NEW BAND...

...GOAT CHEESE PIZZA!

HI DAD

HOW DID THE CAROLING GO AT THE NURSING HOME, GUYS?

SORT OF OKAY, KIND OF, I GUESS.

SCOTT and BORGMAN

THEY WERE GLAD TO SEE US AND STUFF, BUT THEY DIDN'T SEEM TO ENJOY THE MUSIC LIKE WE THOUGHT THEY WOULD.

THAT'S ODD. PEOPLE USUALLY LOVE CHRISTMAS MUSIC.

WELL, THEN, MAYBE **THAT** WAS THE PROBLEM...

MERR

116

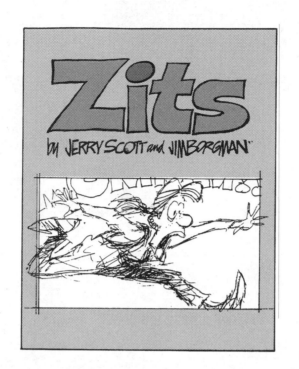

CHRISTMAS VACATION!

OH YEAH!

TWO SOLID WEEKS OF FREEDOM, SOLITUDE, RELAXATION......

SCOTT and BORGMAN

...AND RELATIVES.

JEREMY, AUNT MARGE DROPPED BY AND SHE BROUGHT THE TWINS!

WE ALREADY WENT IN YOUR ROOM AND TOUCHED ALL YOUR STUFF.

My AUNT MARGE...

JEREMY!

BIG.... LOUD..... KISSY....

LOOK HOW TALL YOU'RE GETTING, HONEY!

C'MERE AND GIVE ME A SMOOCH!

SCOTT and BORGMAN

UH... SNICKER-DOODLE?

OOH!

...and, LUCKY FOR ME, EASILY DIVERTED.

CONNIE, IS THIS REAL BUTTER?

The BAD THING ABOUT CHRISTMAS VACATION IS THAT RELATIVES ARE ALWAYS COMING OVER.

THE GOOD THING IS that THEY EVENTUALLY LEAVE.

KIDS! IT'S TIME TO GO!

YES!

THE BAD THING IS that THERE SEEMS TO BE A NEVER-ENDING SUPPLY OF THEM.

BYE!

HI!

NO-O-O-O-O-O-O-O-O-O!

SCOTT and BORGMAN

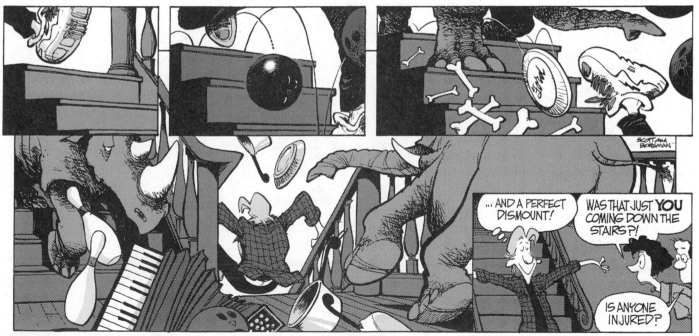